100 Great Podcasting
Tips

From 100 Great Podcasters

Compiled By Gary Leland

———

Edited By Travis Littig

ISBN-13: 9781517143398

ISBN-10: 151714339X

Printed in the United States of America

Table of Contents

Preface

I personally discovered the world of podcasting in 2004, and have enjoyed every moment. I believe I was probably one of the first 100 podcasters on the planet. In 2006, I received an award from Time Magazine for my website, PodcastPickle.com. It was selected as one of the "50 Coolest Websites" in the world.

When I attended a social media event in Las Vegas in 2014, someone addressed me as a podcasting pioneer. I do not think I qualify as a pioneer but was truly humored with the compliment.

Podcasting has given me great insight into a multitude of topics. Podcasting has increased my business, fostered new friendships, and enhanced my life more than I ever thought it could. I am grateful podcasting has opened new chapters in my journey of life.

I have asked my growing network of podcast experts, friends, and contributors to present one piece of advice. I am pleased to share their experience and knowledge about the podcasting industry with you.

- Gary Leland

Acknowledgements

I would like to personally thank each of the individuals represented in this book for their contributions to this collection of advice, knowledge, and inspiration. I hope this information will help you to take the next step in your podcasting adventure.

This information was gathered from the growing community of podcasters and would not be possible without their support. I want to include a special thank you to Rob Walch, of *podcast411.com*, and Todd Cochran, of *blubrry.com*.

I have been inspired by others to put together a helpful resource tool for the new, growing, or experienced podcaster. I sincerely hope the information in this book will trigger greatness in whatever avenue you pursue as a podcaster.

Thank You!

Questions About Podcasting?

Here are some of the most common questions about podcasting:

1. **What is Podcasting?**
   Podcasting was developed as a way to automatically send audio and video files via the Internet. These files are most commonly broken up in episodic content that is delivered on a consistent schedule. Users can stream or download an audio or video podcast from well known sources such as iTunes, Stitcher, or a podcaster's website. The user may listen to or watch this digital media file on any device that can access the file. You may use a laptop, desktop, mobile phone, or tablet. In the early days of podcasting, you could only use a portable media player such as an iPod.

2. **What is a Podcast feed?**
   A podcast feed is a URL to a RSS (rich site summary) file in XML format. A RSS feed, is a source of online content available in a stream. In the context of a podcast, it can be used to automatically download new episodes when they become available. XML is a format for creating content on the Internet. When a user subscribes to a podcast's RSS feed using a "podcatcher", then that user will receive automatic digital media content updates. Another name for podcatcher, is known as a feed aggregator.

3. **What is a Podcatcher?**

A podcatcher is an application that you can use to subscribe to podcasts. Podcatcher programs, like iTunes for example, will automatically download podcasts as they are posted to the podcast provider's audio hosting site. Each podcaster must submit their RSS feed to the podcatcher service for approval.

4. **What is a Podcaster, and who makes Podcasts?**

"Podcaster" is a term that was developed over the years to refer to the host, author and/or producer of a podcast. Podcasters can range from a professional broadcaster to a DIY content creator from the office or extra space of his/her home.

5. **What is the difference between a Podcast and Streaming Media?**

Previously, a podcast was downloaded once in it's entirety, and was playable by the user at any time, without Internet connection. Streaming media, refers to a continuous transmission of data received by a user who is connected to the source of that data, like a television or radio broadcast. But today, with services and mobile devices able to connect to the web at much faster speeds, most shows are able to be streamed on a device.

6. **How do I upload my Podcast to iTunes?**

This step confuses many, because iTunes does not host your content, they only "pull" your content hosted on a server or other service (recommended in the Podcast Tools chapter of this book.) After you have your media hosted, you will be given or create an RSS feed and that is what you submit through an iTune account. Find more here: *www.apple.com/ itunes/podcasts/*

7. What are Show Notes?

Podcasts today expanded from only using the simple description area of their mp3 meta data to describe their show. To Podcasters who feature full blog style writing which cover the information contained in each episode of your podcast, links, images, videos, resources, and more. Many Podcasts today have their full episode transcribed and placed on their blog or website for SEO purposes.

8. Why do I need podcast cover art?

High quality cover art attracts new subscribers to your podcast, gives a tone and feeling to what your show is about, and a simple title and tagline of your show. This allows users to pick out what they are interested in when searching through podcasts. Cover art must be in the JPEG or PNG file formats and in the RGB color space with a minimum size of 1400 x 1400 pixels and a maximum size of 3000 x 3000 pixels.

9. What is New & Noteworthy?

When launching a new podcast, one of the biggest ways to gain traction in your launch phase, is to take advantage of the New and Noteworthy Section of iTunes. This is a highly coveted spot in the iTunes Store directory which puts your show in front of millions of users, and allows you to be highly visible for an amazing 8 weeks. To start ranking you must upload at least 5 episodes before launch. You should ask your circle of influence to download, subscribe, and leave a review as soon as they see the podcast show up in the iTunes Podcast Directory. There is no magic formula for this process, just good 'ole fashion word of mouth marketing.

10. **How do I make money from my Podcast?**

That can be a hard question to answer with many variables, I recommend going to the "Podcasts About Podcasting" chapter of this book to find expert advice from the community.

History Of Podcasting - The Beginning

The true godfathers of podcasting are Dave Winer and Adam Curry. Dave Winer is a software developer, RSS evangelist, and developer of the popular weblog package Radio Userland, (radio.userland.com). Today he produces Morning Coffee Notes and Trade Secrets (secrets.scripting.com), Adam Curry produces the wildly popular Daily Source Code (live.curry.com). Adam is well known as mid-80s former MTV VJ.

Podcasting started, before the term was even invented, with an idea from a meeting in 2000 between Adam and Dave. The two were talking about automated media distribution. The conversation centered around video rather than audio. Dave was against the idea of a subscription-based system for video downloads.

Remember this was 2000 before the world-wide leap in the number of Broadband Internet connections. Dave felt the Internet simply had not evolved to the point where it would support large video downloads, not to mention the cost of delivering content. His analogy was that it was taking longer to download video than it was to play it, and many times the video was poor quality and you really did not know what you were going to get.

Adam's idea was to look at Internet connections differently and to consider all of the bandwidth that goes to waste when you are not using your Internet connection. He wanted a software solution that could download items that he subscribed to. This really wasn't a new idea, but there were no tools to do this in the fashion they desired.

Dave was already working on Real Simple Syndication (RSS). The site: http://webreference.com/authoring/languages/xml/rss/intro/ offers a detailed discussion of this exciting lightweight XML format. RSS is specifically designed for creating new stories. It enables you to share headings and other Web content across the Internet. Because an RSS text file can include dynamic content as well as static content, you can use it to distribute new content from your site to others.

Dave had made some revisions to the original RSS 0.91 specification developed by Netscape and formalized RSS 2.0 in 2003. The RSS 2.0 standard was released by Harvard under a Creative Commons license.

In the meantime, Dave wanted to come up with a format to deliver content via a subscription system. So he thought the process would need to be broken into three problems:

What software do you use when creating the content?
What software reads the content?
Where do you find the content?

These three elements needed to come together to make the vision developed at that meeting in 2000 happen.

Until the summer of 2004, progress was slow and, even though many of the individual pieces were there in place, they were not all tied together until Adam decided to try his hand at programming and developed the first rudimentary podcatcher application with Apple Scripts.

Dave initially thought that what Adam had created would not work, but with his hacked together Apple Script, Adam was able to capture and download the audio post that Dave embedded in his weblog.

Adam's program read Dave's RSS feed and downloaded the audio file. Adam's "podcatcher" program was looking for items within Dave's RSS feed known as enclosures. The program simply grabbed the file within these enclosures, downloaded it, and then utilizing the API released for iTunes, put the file in his iTunes playlist, which then could be synced to his iPod.

Dave and Adam worked for four years after that original meeting to make subscription and automatic file downloads of video and audio content easy for the masses. Things seem to always come full circle and by a little luck in that we had a quasi celebrity promoting what they had accomplished, Adam's simple Apple Script lit a fire for the development of podcasting, which is in full swing today.

Adam Curry says, "Podcasting is where developers and users party together." This has been a profound battle cry and has resulted in amazing achievements in a short time. The momentum behind podcasting is simply amazing. The number of people racing to make it easier to produce and consume podcasts is going on at a frenzied pace with at least a dozen teams bringing software products that are largely free to the market place. The Open Source community and the initial innovations and foresight of Adam and Dave were the keys to the explosive growth and initial creation of software tools that sky rocketed the growth of this medium. Today teams of individuals collaborate to bring new features to the software tools we are going to discuss in detail.

By early 2005, new media creators were jumping into the space and a number of podcast directories started to emerge to support the cataloging of podcasts being created. One of the most popular at the time was PodcastAlley.com and later PodcastPickle.com.

In January of 2005, the first podcast network appeared at techpodcasts.com, which today is a property of RawVoice. Other networks such as The Podcast Network began to emerge. Some of these networks were topic focused and others carried a wide variety of content.

In May of 2005, Todd Cochrane the CEO of RawVoice, brought into the podcasting space the very first major advertiser. His advertising deal with GoDaddy.com proved to be a maturing point in the space when people realized that they could make a full-time living creating new media and distributing it as a podcast.

In July of 2005 Apple introduced Podcasting Support into iTunes and an explosion of new listeners and new media creators jumped into the space. This is also about the time that mainstream media started to understand the power of automated delivery of media content and very quickly you had new media creators content and main stream media content being given equal billing on iTunes.

In August of 2005, the inaugural People's Choice Podcast Awards were held in Ontario, Calif., during the first Podcast Expo. The next year in 2006 Time Magazine named my website PodcastPickle.com as one of the 50 coolest websites in the world. From this point on a number of companies jumped into the podcasting space and several have been venture funded. With the majority of those companies, business models are built around advertising revenue in podcasting.

Source: History courtesy of Todd Cochrane © 2015 Blubrry Podcasting Community - (*www.Blubrry.com*)

Reasons To Start Podcasting

1. **Be Seen as an Expert**

   Podcasting gives you the opportunity to share your message directly to the listener. The intimate and direct nature of a podcast allows greater trust in the host over a radio or tv broadcast.

2. **More Leads - More Sales**

   A targeted niche market is great for generating a subscriber list and have listeners that are actually interested in what you share with them.

3. **Reach a Global Audience**

   Even the smallest podcaster has the ability to reach a worldwide audience. With the internet and growth of technology almost everyone has access to listen to audio content.

4. **Make Money from Your Show**

   Having the ability to grow and control your own audience, gives you the freedom to be selective in ad space or to advertise your own products.

5. **Become the Media**

As a podcaster you have the ability to become a source of news and information for your audience. They will become avid listeners and come to you first to get the scoop on your industry. You are the expert.

6. Podcasting is Inexpensive to Start Up

With the advancement of mobile phones today, and the advent of numerous podcasting apps, you can easily begin podcasting on little to no investment.

7. To Build A Targeted Audience

As you begin to release content and build a community around your concept. People will come to your show for specific reasons. As you drive traffic to your mailing list or website, this allows you to create something for people to share and join in.

8. Promote Your Own Products or Services

When you have an audience consistently checking back in for new releases, this allows you to pinpoint your products and services to exactly what they are looking for. You have the opportunity to create a demand for your product

9. It's an Emerging Content Platform

Podcasting has grown in many ways since its

inception. When new shows develop, podcasters become more creative in the content they produce. This is your chance to create something big!

10. Increase the Size of your Network

Struggling to find ways to grow your following, and reach more people with your message? This is your chance to talk directly to millions of people around the world. Don't be shy.

11. Connect with Professionals in Your Industry

This is your chance to interview and rub shoulders with the cream of the crop in your industry. As podcasting continues to grow in popularity, more people understand how important it is to be interviewed and get their message out.

12. Another Way To Repurpose Your Content

Take videos and other content you have already created, extract the audio mp3 file and repurpose it with new blog posts, social media, and market it. Bring life into old content!

100 Great Podcasting Tips

What advice would you give a podcaster that is just starting out?

1. Rob Walch - "Today in iOS"

twitter.com/podcast411

Get your own personalized smartphone App for your show. You need one for iOS, Android, and Windows Phone 8. There is a lot of talk about getting your show out everywhere - but there is no BIGGER anywhere then the App stores. Each month over 1.5 Billion people download apps from the iTunes App Store, Google Play App Store, Amazon App Store, and Windows Phone 8 App store. If you do not have an app for your show - you are not going to be discovered by these app downloaders. And on the Android side the ONLY way to be discovered natively on Android as a Podcaster is if you have an App for your show.

Edison research found that over 75% of podcast consumers consume less than 5 different podcast series. Having a stand alone app for your show - makes it easier for the majority of listeners to consume your show - and it helps build your brand with your listeners. And lets face facts - it makes you look more committed to your show.

———

2. Todd Cochrane - "Geek News Central"

twitter.com/geeknews

New podcasters need to understand that building an audiences trust does not happen overnight. It takes time and hard work. Rome was not built in a day, and you should expect a couple of years of doing weekly or twice weekly shows at a minimum to really grow your show.

Do not worry about new and notable, worry about having compelling, engaging content. If you are able to connect with you audience on a one on one basis even though you are talking to the masses you will be well on your way to success.. I always tell new podcasters give your show two years at a minimum to really grow your audience.

———

3. Dave Jackson - "School of Podcasting"

twitter.com/learntopodcast

Start with ONE podcast and break your launch into bite size chunks. Come up with your podcasts's name, then your format, then your microphone,etc. If you look at the overall process it can be a bit intimidating, but when you break it into bite size chunks, your focus will get you through the process. Once it's launched, it is much easier to keep it going.

———

4. Rob Greenlee - "The New Media Show"

twitter.com/robgreenlee

It should always be the goal to get your first few episodes to be perfect, but the reality is that few will be listening yet. So, be patient and realize that podcasting for most is a marathon not a sprint. Be always improving and listen to your listeners as over time they will help you shape your show into something you and your audience will love.

———

5. John Lee Dumas - "Entrepreneur On Fire"

twitter.com/johnleedumas

Define your UVD. Unique Value Distinguisher. What specific value are you going to provide via your Podcast that is going to distinguish you uniquely from other Podcasts in your niche? Decide upon your UVD, focus, and IGNITE!

———

6. Michael Stelzner - "Social Media Marketing Podcast"

twitter.com/mike_stelzner

It's important to ask this question: "How will this podcast help me accomplish... (blank)." And then fill in the blank. Is your show designed to help you get more exposure in your industry, book more clients, sell your event or something else? Have a real clear understanding of what you hope to accomplish before you jump in. Also ask yourself, "How will I know if I'm making progress?" Come up with some simple triggers, such as emails from listeners or reviews on iTunes. Thinking about these things in advance will fuel you when the going gets tough, and it will.

———

7. Lynette Young - "Finding Your Fierce"

twitter.com/LynetteRadio

No matter what your intentions, treat your show like a business. Your listeners will come to value your show as a part of their life and business. Don't disrespect the time they give you in order to listen to your show.

———

8. Paul Colligan - "The Podcast Report"

twitter.com/Colligan

7 Steps To A Better Show

1. Expensive Audio Programs Will No More Make You A Better Podcaster Than An Expensive Knife Will Make You A Better Chef.
2. Reaching Your Audience Is More Important Than Your Format.
3. People Come For The Podcast Content, They Stay For The Podcast Voice.

4. Are You Responding To What Podcasting Is - Or What You Hope It Will Become?
5. The Message Makes The Podcast More Than The Tech Ever Will.
6. Evergreen Content Is Almost Always A Better Monetization Strategy.
7. If You Don't Know What You Want, You're Not Going To Get It.

---

9. Dan Franks - "Men Seeking Tomahawks"

twitter.com/dmfranks

Take all advice you get with a grain of salt. Ultimately the best thing about podcasting is that there are no rules, therefore you can do whatever you want!

---

10. Mitch Todd - "Chocolate at Midnight"

twitter.com/mediamitch

A first-time listener to your podcast may only listen for a couple of minutes before deciding whether or not they will listen to the entire show. It is important that you listen critically to the first few minutes of your show and make sure you 1) get their attention, 2) clearly explain what your show and this episode is about, and 3) describe the benefit they will receive by listening. Have others listen to the first few minutes of your podcast and give you feedback.

11. Erik J. Fisher - "Beyond The To-Do List"

twitter.com/ErikJFisher

Don't worry about the show notes. Your audience wants to hear your next episode more than read your new show notes. Release the show! Polish the show notes later if you must.

12. Mike Russell - "Audio Production Show"

twitter.com/imikerussell

Make sure you focus on your audio quality. The top 100 podcasts all have great production values and so should your podcast. 30 seconds is all it takes for someone to decide if they will keep listening or not so make that intro count!

13. Evo Terra - "The Opportunistic Travelers Podcast"

twitter.com/evoterra

"How long should my podcast be?" is looking at the problem the wrong way. The right questions is "how short can I make my podcast"?

Make it as short as you possibly can. People decide NOT to listen to podcasts every day because they don't have the time. But no one ever unsubscribed to a show because the episodes were too short.

———

14. Jeremy Vest - "Vidpow Tube Talk"

twitter.com/vidpowbam

Get started! Don't wait until you have enough episodes, ideas or guests turn on your mic and go! You can figure out what your listeners need and want as it builds and grows. Also don't launch and wait for people to start listening. Building your audience is about a million times harder for most of us then the podcast its-self.

Its best not to be anything but yourself and only speak on your biggest passions. Most podcasters that I've met are tech nerds, my advice is to buy a simple, nice USB mic and focus on the content. And finally with billions of video views a day on Facebook and YouTube don't forget to turn on a camera to take advantage of video platforms.

———

15. Jessica Kupferman - "She Podcasts"

twitter.com/jesskupferman

Commitment is key. Choose a schedule for your show and stick to it no matter what! Your listeners will come to depend on .and rely on your show. Don't disappoint!

———

16. Christopher Gronlund -
"Men in Gorilla Suits"

twitter.com/cgronlund

Do the podcast you'd still do if only 10 people listened. That's the show that's in your heart; that's the show you must do. Anything less is fabrication. If your podcast is from the heart before it's about numbers or sponsorship or anything else, you've already won.

———

17. Tim Gillette - "The Tim Gillette Radio Show"

twitter.com/rockerlifecoach

Schedule your first show and just do it. Do not wait until you get everything perfect. In the beginning you are not going to have lots of listeners so use that time to find your niche. From blogging to business starting, I always just got started and built as I went.

———

18. Ben Krueger - "Cashflow Podcasting"

Start with the end in mind. If you're podcasting to spread a message, build an audience or build a brand, always have clear direction of where you're going and what you have to offer listeners before getting started. Armed with this purpose of direction, you'll be able to keep the listeners' interest your highest priority and develop an audience of raving fans that will truly connect with your message, your community, and you.

————

19. Erin Smith - "The Starters Club"

twitter.com/TheStartersClub

Use preset questions as a guide, but not a must to get through your episodes. Instead, be open to where the conversation goes. If you force yourself to follow a list of questions, it can be awkward trying to figure out a way to circle back to them. Listen, engage, and just be open to the natural path of the conversation.

————

20. Jeffrey Powers - "Geekazine Review"

twitter.com/geekazine

If your goal is to get people to listen/watch your content, then make a plan to promote before you launch - Just like a TV or radio show would do - 30 to 60 days before. This doesn't mean buying ad time, but it can mean spending some time on message boards helping others and moderately promoting it. Do your major promotions in your ABOUT section of Facebook, Twitter, LinkedIn and more. That includes the about section of whatever board you signed up for.

It's also a good idea to collect your business cards and get a small "one-time" email list together. Use a service like MailChimp to organize and send the email.

Free press release is another great way to promote. When you put in contact information, set up an email like PR@yourpodcastwebsite.com . This will float all PR information to that address and also make companies think you have a PR team behind you.

Continuity is always a great practice, no better way to get it started than to start right now and work the plan.

––––––––

21. Mike Dell - "Podcast Help Desk"

twitter.com/mgdell

Own your own brand. Your RSS feed, Website and content are yours. Don't let 3rd parties control any of that. When promoting your podcast, point them to your own domain name, not iTunes, Stitcher or any other website other than your own. Services may come and go so if you are running everything from your own domain, you will always be in control of your content.

––––––––

22. Tee Morris - "The Shared Desk"

twitter.com/TeeMonster

Record at least five shows discussing evergreen (not dated, timeless) topics, edit them, and get them ready for posting, but keep them in reserve. That way, if something comes up and prevents you from recording an episode, you can record a quick introduction and then post a show, staying on track with a production schedule.

————

23. Jonny Andrews - "Audience Hacker"

twitter.com/JonnyAndrewsX

Don't be afraid to screw it all up. Just about every show that builds a following and makes an impact started somewhere other than where it now is. Just pick an idea, layout a basic plan and put one foot in front of the other until it either works or breaks. If it breaks make a few modifications and go back to pushing forward. Don't fear mistakes. They are what make you in the end.

————

24. Jeff Brown - "Read to Lead Podcast"

twitter.com/thejeffbrown

Answer why you're doing it in the first place. Then, articulate this "why" in the form of a Worldview through which your content is filtered. This will give your listener something she can identify with. Use it to draw a line in the sand; dare her to cross it and embark on this journey with you.

---

25. James Kinson - "Cash Car Convert Show"

twitter.com/cashcarconvert

Getting "A" listers on your show won't make your show take off with explosive growth. I thought it would for my show, but it didn't. My show grew as I created good solid content over a period of months. Great content created consistently overtime will grow your audience. "A" listers are great social proof for a show, but your content is what grows a show.

---

26. Anthony Tran - "Marketing Access Pass"

twitter.com/AnthonyTranMAP

Podcasting has been the single biggest catalyst for my business growth. The advice that I want to share with you is that you have to look at your podcast as an amazing communication tool. Podcasting gives you the ability to share your thoughts, ideas, and message to people all around the world. It is also the greatest platform to help you connect with your listeners, peers, and influencers.

By focusing on building relationships new doors and opportunities will open up for you. These opportunities will skyrocket your business to the next level. Thus, don't look at your downloads numbers as numbers, but rather as people who you can have strong business relationships with. Join The Movement!

_____

27. Steve Stewart - "MoneyPlan SOS"

twitter.com/MoneyPlanSOS

Don't Sweat It: We often place high expectations on new things. Think back to your last home improvement project - it took longer and cost more than you had expected. The same can be true for podcasting.

It takes a while to find your voice, the audience will not automatically appear, and the message behind your show will likely change.

It took 23 episodes before I discovered my motto: Pay Attention - Not Interest. Since then my show has changed course and I have found my niche.

Your 86th episode will sound different from Episode 001. Don't sweat perfection when you are getting started, just keep your audience's needs in mind every time you hit record and they will come back to listen again and again.

_____

28. Lance Anderson - "Verge of the Fringe"

twitter.com/1LanceAnderson

My "advice" for the creative and artistically inclined podcasts: Do your own thing. Fans can be fickle, so you have to create a podcast that has meaning to you first and foremost. Too much attention is placed on how will the audience react, will they continue to subscribe? Don't worry about them, sure it's great to get cool feedback, but you shouldn't build your podcast around what other people think.

Also the podcast experts are invested in you doing things their way, it reaffirms what they are selling. Use the advice that is helpful, but always "follow your bliss" as the late great Joseph Campbell often said.

―――――

29. Sarah Mitchell - "Brand Newsroom"

twitter.com/globalcopywrite

Stick with it. Consistency gets easier over time so force yourself in the beginning to release a new episode on a regular basis. Make sure your audience knows when to expect to find your new content and don't let them down.

―――――

30. Joel Boggess - "ReLaunch!"

twitter.com/JoelBoggess

Don't "accidentally" or "quietly" release your podcast.

Set your goal(s) for the show; Have an understanding of what you're trying to accomplish with it;

Give yourself a runway in preparation of the show's launch and a specific blastoff date; Build a system to generate immediate subscribers, ratings, and reviews. (Secret sauce to the iTunes ratings game.)

My specific goal was to hit #1 in iTunes "New and Noteworthy" in all of our categories; I knew doing so, would be a huge door opener for me. Which it turned out to be in multiple ways.

Depending on how far along you already are in your podcasting journey, one-two months ramp-up time is plenty.

Unfortunately, I see shows with none or very few listener comments and ratings, and hosts struggling to get them. And it makes me cringe because with just a little forethought and planning, it doesn't have to be that way.

Building and developing a launch team (friends, family, supporters) was the #1 difference-maker in ReLaunch's quick ratings success, strong standing during it's debut season, and a ten-fold increase in listenership over the course of twelve months.

———

31. Travis Littig - "Skate To Create Podcast"

twitter.com/skate_to_create

Can you hear me? What is that sound? Is that a dog in the background?

Audio.... Some say content is king, some say quality is key. I say, turn on the recorder and start talking! Stop worrying if you can create the most original content on the market. Stop slaving over your audio tracks for the best sounding show on earth. You are not going to have it. Just produce content and gain experience and knowledge of how to produce more shows better, faster, and more consistent.

———

32. Vernon Ross - "The Social Strategy Podcast"

twitter.com/rosspr

Your audience deserves the best show you can give so before you get on the mic do your research. It's never a good idea to be wrong about the facts on a guest. Take the time to Google the person in advance of the interview if you are an interview based show. It shows that person that you care enough about them to know what they are working on, the correct title of their book if it's an author etc. If you are not interview based have notes for the subject you're covering so you can stay on track with your episode. So above all be prepared your audience really deserves your best work.

———

33. Dwain Scott - "SHIFTing WORK"

twitter.com/leanmeleanu

Get Over Yourself!

You are the only thing holding you back from starting. Get in front of the mic and hit record! Stop making excuses, they don't move but you can. In podcasting motion is everything start and keep moving forward. You will grow and improve weather you start today or next year. Don't wait and get over yourself!

————

34. Jay "PodVader" Soderberg - "Next Fan Up"

twitter.com/therealpodvader

Focus on building your bad ass clubhouse. Make it as bad ass as you possibly can. The more bad ass it is, the more people will want to join - including sponsors. Don't worry about that as you start - just focus on that clubhouse.

————

35. Joe Saul-Sehy - "Stacking Benjamins"

twitter.com/AverageJoeMoney

Your format is the key to success. While you may think that interviewing guests about "them" is the key to success, long time listeners keep coming back because of "you." Make sure an infuse enough of "you" in your show.

That said, also remember that new listeners come for information, not to hear about how awesome your weekend was (unless you host the "My Awesome Weekend Podcast"....then forget this advice!). For that reason, get to the meat quickly at the beginning, but use the entire show to build rapport and to stray slightly off topic. If you're going to build community, do it at the END of your podcast. By then, you've already delivered value to them with the contents of your show AND the only people who stick around for the full show are normally your biggest fans anyway.

Finally....throw off discouragement! A podcast IS sometimes another job. Remember you're a professional, and a lot of people (your listeners) are counting on you being there for them. If you're podcasting because you love having a message for listeners, that should keep you fired up and ready to put together another episode! Good luck!

————

36. Jared Easley - "Starve the Doubts"

twitter.com/jaredeasley

Be the Noticer! Every podcaster wants their show to get noticed & attract listeners. The best way to get noticed is to start by noticing! Notice your target listeners & get to know them. Noticing them in a generous & authentic way will create rapport. Rapport overtime will naturally yield Reciprocity over time. Reciprocity that is compounded creates an army. When multiple people say that they love your show & what you are doing... others will hear that & want to know what the hype is all about (aka. the army). If you want your podcast to get noticed... start by being the noticer.

————

37. John Dennis - "Smart Time Online"

Producing quality content takes more time than beginner podcasters typically realize. What you might think takes an hour to do, double it. If you can afford to outsource the mundane things like editing audio, do it.

———

38. Dan Miller - "48 Days"

twitter.com/48DaysTeam

Listen to your own show, again and again. Ask yourself if you would be excited as a new listener. Are you overusing filler words (um, ya know, basically, actually, etc.)? Are you clearing your throat or coughing? Are you giving your guests ample time to respond?   Are you prepared with music clips, intros, and resources? Don't use informality as an excuse for sloppiness.

———

39. Tim Paige - "ConversionCast"

twitter.com/TimThePaige

Be unique. There are a gazillion podcasts out there and a gazillion slight variations on those topics. Really make your show stand out in a real way.

———

40. James Manning - "Skate To Create Podcast"

twitter.com/Royal_Deca

Start today. Listen to as many podcasts as possible in the beginning. Eventually, you will start to record more than actually listening to other podcasts.

―――――

41. Jesse Jackson - "Storming the Castle"

twitter.com/jessejacksondfw

Podcast about something you enjoy. Try to have a format that allows your listeners to feel comfortable listening to the show. Don't be afraid to change up the format when needed. Have fun if you aren't enjoying talking about the subject, they won't like listening to the podcast.

―――――

42. Scott Voelker - "The Amazing Seller Podcast"

twitter.com/ScottVoelker

1. Pick a topic you love and want to learn more about. It's not about knowing everything, it's about learning and reporting what you learn through experience.

2. Be consistent with your content. No less than 1 show per week. I currently do 3 shows per week. Create a schedule and stick to it.

3. Batch your recordings. Outline the bullets and topics, then record a batch. You want to get in the groove and stay there for the duration.

4. Be yourself and don't worry about being perfect. If you make mistakes...laugh about them and show that you are a real person. Being transparent is key to Building trust.

5. Buy a decent mic to represent quality. Even if your show is not perfect, good sound makes it ok and people will still feel it's good quality. You will hold the attention...rather than having your audience annoyed that the sound is terrible.

The Bottom Line is...Take Action and you'll GET RESULTS!

———

43. Ted Ryce - "Legendary Life Podcast"

twitter.com/LegendaryLifeP

The best 3 tips that I can give a podcaster that is just starting are:

1. Get Started

Most of your show prep, interviewing skills, etc will be learned on the job. You can read, watch webinars and listen to podcasts about how to do a great podcast. But eventually you're going to have to have the courage to get started. You will mess up. You will have technical issues. You will do less-than-stellar interviews. And that's all okay. It's part of the process

What isn't okay is to put off starting your podcast because of fear you will make a mistake or not be good enough. Don't worry. Unless you have a background in public speaking or are just a natural communicator (I was not either of these by the way) then you won't be that great when you start. But you will get better. As long as you keep going and don't give up. So start as soon as you can and begin building your podcasting knowledge and skill.

2. Strive for Excellence

Make sure that you strive for excellence in every area of podcasting. Invest in the best audio equipment you can. Then upgrade when you can. Invest in learning public speaking to become a master at communicating. Join toastmasters. Join an Improv Acting class. Take courses. Listen to top podcasts to learn best podcasting practices and to get inspired. Listen to the masters of mainstream media to see what you can glean from what they do. How they talk. How they structure their content. No matter what your style or format is, stay hungry and strive to be the best you can be at your podcast.

3. Find Your Authentic Voice

Too many podcasters sound the same. Their voice may be different, but the structure of their show, the guests they interview and the questions they ask those guests sound the same.

This is perhaps the best piece of advice I can give to podcasters who have already started. Make sure you pay attention to trends, but also find your unique voice in the process. You can emulate other podcasters style and organization but never copy them.

A great way to set yourself apart, it to become a more interesting person. Most people are just not that interesting. But you can become more interesting by traveling more, learning new skills, taking up new hobbies, attending events outside of internet marketing and podcasting. Those are just a few examples. Not only will they make you more interesting but those experiences will also give you stories you can tell to connect better with your audience. Feel free to come up with your own and follow your unique path. Just make sure that you commit yourself to becoming the most interesting person you can be.

---

44. Eric Tivers - "ADHD reWired"

twitter.com/LegendaryLifeP

If I could go back in time, I would have spent much less time editing. As a musician, I value good sounding audio, but spending 10 hours editing a 45-minute episode is outrageous, but that is what I did. Over time, I left in more and more of the mistakes. Not only that, I would spend hours tweaking audio frequencies. These are changes that nobody would even notice but me. It was fun, but was not what I should be doing. I finally decided to hire an editor. I wish I did it sooner.

The other piece of advice is to let your podcast evolve. It's good to communicate what listeners can expect, but you can change that if you want. Make sure you are having fun with it. And if you're getting bored with it, give yourself permission to take changes with changing things up.

And be real. Be open. Be yourself. Don't try to be like another podcast. Don't use the same format, or same questions as other podcasters do. And as a host, listen to your guest. Put away your prepared questions, and listen to your guest. Have a conversation. Help your guest tell their story.

———

45. Kirk Bowman - "Art of Value Show"

twitter.com/ArtOfValue

When your budget allows, invest in an external compressor/gate. This will help eliminate background noise when you are not speaking like computer fans, dogs barking, etc. The dbx 266XS is a 2-channel compressor/gate that is usually available for $100.

———

46. Jaime Jay - "Podcast Professors"

twitter.com/podprofessors

One of the best things you can do when you are getting started is to make sure that you understand what your message is and who are sharing your message with. While this may seem easy, it's definitely worth taking the time to think it through.

Figure out exactly what your message is so that you don't confuse anyone. People will tune into you because they like, love and trust you, but if you are providing information they are interested in on a consistent basis, they will lose interest.

You also need to understand who it is you are talking to. This is incredibly important because you can craft your message and deliver it to your ideal listener. Too many people make the mistake of trying to share their message with a large audience in the beginning. Niche down and pretend as if you are talking to your friend (obviously, don't use that person's name).

You will notice that your message comes across more conversational. This helps to create more interesting story telling and before you know it, your audience will identify with your message and your podcast will continue to grow.

———

47. Rick Coste - "Evolution Talk"

twitter.com/rickcoste

I have two pieces of advice.

One. Consume podcasts. Just as many professional writers urge aspiring writers to read, and to read a lot, the same goes for creating audio content. Not a day, or a show, goes by that I don't learn something new. If you ever think you know all there is to know - you don't. Consume podcasts about podcasting as well as those that interest you or that share your genre and format. Your show will be so much better for it.

Two. Spot check your show prior to publishing the final work. I learned this the hard way... twice! Had I taken my own advice and listened to the show before publishing it I wouldn't have scrambled to upload a corrected version, nor would I have been worried about listeners who may have downloaded the 'corrupt' version. Now I give the show a quick listen to make sure the levels are right, the music isn't overpowering, and that there are't any unwanted gaps.

Three (yes, I know I said two). Have fun!!!!!

---

48. David V. Kimball - "Beyond Tweeting"

twitter.com/davidvkimball

Listen to yourself. Then strike the "uh" and "you know" from your vocabulary!

---

49. Bob Harper -
"The Dukes of Startup Podcast"

twitter.com/bobcharper

Just start. Commit to it and get started. Start recording, start interviewing, start writing, and you will figure everything out from there.

---

50. Chris Mcneill - "Amazing Workplace"

twitter.com/ChrisEMcneill

Do background research on your guests! Check out their Twitter and Facebook feeds, and see what they've been up to outside the interview topic. This makes for great pre-chat material and can break down barriers and get them comfortable chatting.

———

51. Jason Stapleton - "The Jason Stapleton Program"

twitter.com/jason_stapleton

Podcasters place a lot of emphasis on the beginning. They concern themselves with getting into things like New & Noteworthy while neglecting the one thing that will do more for the success than anything else. Persistence.

Success is built through years of hard work. By the dedicated professional who continues to press on even when his world is collapsing down around him and everyone he talks to is telling him to hang it up. History will judge you by how you finish. No one is going to remember or care if you made it into the top 10 in New & Noteworthy if you give up 3 months later. Focus on the end, on the goal. Then work like hell to make it happen.

———

52. Nic Hayes - "Brand Newsroom"

Clear your mind of any expectations and be prepared to be patient as any success you might have will take a minimum 12 months to see come into fruition. Be yourself and don't try and emulate another as this is what people are looking for. Authenticity is really your only asset when starting out so make sure you're being true to yourself and the audience you are engaging with.

———

53. Byron Ingraham - "The Big Movement"

twitter.com/byroningraham

Get started. It's better to take action than to wait to get things perfect. You will make mistakes, but you will make many great strides in launching your podcast.

———

54. Nuchtchas - "Nutty Bites"

twitter.com/Nuchtchas

Never use a free service. Granted there are free options, but may site that offer podcasting free with paid perks can end up holding your podcast hostage. If you can't pay for hosting, go through archieve.org, never one of those other sites. They are predatory.

Always control your own RSS feed, if you are podcasting from your own domain, make your rss your domain.

Always use your own domain for everything! When you give out the email, use the domain's email.

Redundancy is a podcasters best friend. If you are podcasting with two or more recording locations, make sure at least two of you are recording. Extra recordings can never hurt.

Listen to your podcast. Listen to it as a listeners, learn from listening You will hear your flaws and learn to fix them.

Don't talk about how long it's been since you last recorded, don't talk about why your show is delayed, don't talk about running out of time.

_____

55. Mimika Cooney - "Mimika Cooney"

twitter.com/mimikacooney

Don't get hung up on the technicalities, instead focus on creating valuable fluff free content people will want to listen to. Avoid the big names with big ego's, the usually don't care to help support your show, instead find guests with meaningful stories and a passion for helping others succeed.

_____

56. Derek Colanduno - "Skepticality"

twitter.com/learntopodcast

Make double sure that you choose a topic that you are sincerely passionate about, and be very open to anyone who might want to help you or provide content which fits your format, or idea. Those things will lessen the possibility that you will start to think that producing your show is 'too much work'.

---

57. Mark Ramsey - "The Tech Tards Show"

twitter.com/markramsey

Just jump in and have fun or you will spend too much time trying to make it perfect.

---

58. Carl LaFlamme - "Carl and Mike"

twitter.com/carlandmike

Make a goal and plan to get highly ranked in iTuned New and Noteworthy for most of your first eight weeks. Do that by setting up a launch team- a group of at least 20 people who will subscribe rate and review you as well as promote you through social media. The extra exposure from New & Noteworthy can help you establish an audience a lot quicker.

---

59. Doug Payton - "Consider This!"

If you're just starting out, just start. You do need to come up with a topic, title, and target audience; the question "What am I going to podcast". But don't get hung up on the equipment; "How a I going to podcast". If you start with your computer's internal mic, free Audacity software to edit, and free WordPress software for your website, that's fine; just get started. The biggest hurdle is the first one. Get good content, and let the audio catch up.

Once you've started, you can deal with the equipment issue later, but getting into the groove of putting out your show is sometimes all you need to feel more comfortable with it. It's easier to get used to the water by jumping right in rather than walking in little by little.

This is not to say that audio quality isn't important; it is. If you can swing the cash for a decent mic, that will be the biggest improvement your audience will hear. But don't wait for perfection before you jump in.

———

60. Mike White - "The Projection Booth"

twitter.com/proboothcast

Think about what you want to say and why you want to say it before diving in. You can always change things around as your show evolves but having a distinct point-of-view up front is invaluable.

———

61. Hank Davis - "Striving Entrepreneur"

twitter.com/HankDavis

Once you set a schedule with your listeners on when your podcast will be released, make sure to stick to that. Think of it as if the listener is your employer. If you don't show up for one day for work, chances are, you're going to get in trouble. On the flip side, if you consistently release your podcast on time, and provide the best content you can, you will be rewarded. Hopefully, not a crappy pen with the companies name on it, but hey... a gift's a gift.

―――――

62. Bandrew Scott - "Podcastage"

twitter.com/podcastage

Once you set a schedule with your listeners on when your podcast will be released, make sure to stick to that. Think of it as if the listener is your employer. If you don't show up for one day for work, chances are, you're going to get in trouble. On the flip side, if you consistently release your podcast on time, and provide the best content you can, you will be rewarded. Hopefully, not a crappy pen with the companies name on it, but hey... a gift's a gift.

―――――

63. Chris Saunders - "Return to Camp Blood"

twitter.com/thecjs0216

Don't be afraid to go full niche. There's a listener out there for every podcast. Don't pay attention to downloads, followers, or subscribers, just grab a mic, a cold beer (or other cold beverage), and talk about your passion with some friends (or with yourself if your friends can't appreciate the level of greatness that is your topic)... the rest will follow!

———

64. Jonathan Powell - "London Arts Review"

twitter.com/FlaneurZine

Go for it! Don't get bogged down in microphones and audio tech. That will all come with practice. Don't procrastinate, just start getting your podcasts out. You will learn far more by doing than by reading about doing. Don't wait until things are perfect. They won't ever be. Good luck!

———

65. Tom Stewart - "A Swift Kick In The Ass"

twitter.com/AKickintheass

A few things I first learned in Radio:

1. Smile. It makes a subtle change in your voice but the listener will pick up on it.

2. "Brevity is the soul of wit." Keep it short and to the point.

3. Ask the listener for only one "Call To Action". Be very specific on what action you want them to perform.

———

66. Andre Kane - "The Electric Radio Show"

twitter.com/studioers

Quit! LOL, No just kidding, just the opposite actually, work very hard and don't give up.This will not happen overnight,but if you stay at it, it will happen.

———

67. Matt Bailey - "Talk For Two"

twitter.com/TalkForTwo

Finding your niche is the most important aspect to starting a podcast. It doesn't matter how good you are or what kind of equipment you have at the start. The great thing about this medium is that shows can be very, very specialized. Find a market that's underserved and serve it. For me, it was Ventriloquism. Now, by no means is my name Marc Maron or Chris Hardwick. However, I have done and seen things I never could have dreamed of all because I was bored and decided to plug my microphone in one summer evening. Any success I've been blessed with comes from serving an under appreciated market that is grateful to have a new resource.

So find your niche and grow out from there. I guarantee you will be surprised.

---

68. Chris Ruggiero -
"The Chris Ruggiero Podcast"

twitter.com/onemanvariety

Stop reading this book and record an episode. Get started and figure it out as you go.

---

69. Dvorah Lansky -
"Podcasting Success Secrets"

twitter.com/MarketingWizard

Schedule a consistent time each week to record your podcast. This will help you to develop a new habit and you'll be able to create new content on a regular basis.

To take the pressure off of yourself, record episodes ahead of time and have 4-6 weeks or more, worth of content ready to publish.

And most importantly, have fun with your podcast. It is a fabulous tool for sharing your wisdom and passion while building relationships with your audience.

---

70. Steve Carmichael - "RunBuzz"

twitter.com/runbuzz

One of the biggest improvements in sound quality came from recording directly into a digital audio recorder like the Zoom or Roland handheld recorders instead of to my computer's hard drive. It helped me eliminate annoying hiss and created a professional sound quality at a much smaller price point than more expensive audio equipment.

————

71. Chel Hamilton - "Meditation Minis"

twitter.com/HypnotistChel

Spend a few hours using a decent keyword research tool like LongTail Pro (paid) or Traffic Travis (free) and see what kinds of thing "real people" are searching for that relate to your show ideas. Then, look at podcasts in iTunes and Stitcher similar to what you want to do and see if there's a hole in the market your podcast can fill.

What's already out there versus what are real people searching to solve or learn? I totally believe the success of my podcast (90k downloads in it's first 3 months, and growing) is because I chose not only meditation (btw - not my first show choice) but because I specifically chose SHORT meditations of 5-10 minutes - all due to my pre-creation research. Find your opportunity - and own it!

————

72. Danny Peña - "Gamertag Radio"

twitter.com/godfree

It's up to you to break the ceiling. Podcasting is the vehicle that can drive you and/or your site to countless opportunities. Don't worry about download numbers. The best promotion is to meet with your community locally. They're the ones that will spread the word about your podcast.

———

73. Alex Thorn - "Live 2 Win Podcast"

twitter.com/Thornfitness

Have a reason WHY you are Podcasting. There is a fan base for every topic, so find yours and stick closely to it.

———

74. Marcy Rosenbaum - "Inside the Entrepreneurial Mind"

twitter.com/entreprenAIR

Create a backlog of shows so you always have a new show "in the bank" and avoid racing against upload deadlines.

———

75. Russ Johns - "RussJohns.com"

twitter.com/RussJohnsDotCom

Please learn how to use your mic by recording in different rooms and environments, listen to the difference and then test different distances and recording levels and find the sound you are searching for. Discover the sound and record several practice sessions so you know what to expect when you launch your first episode.

---

76. Kamala Chambers - "Thriving Launch"

twitter.com/KamalaChambers

One of the best ways to get on New and Noteworthy is to make sure that you have as many ratings and reviews as possible as soon as you launch. Before your podcast even goes live, build anticipation and excitement to your friends, family, social media networks and email lists. Create an Facebook event around the launch of your show.

Offer to give away a free gift to everyone who leaves you a positive rating and review. In the event description, be sure to list out step-by-step instruction on how to rate, review and subscribe so it's as easy as possible. The Thriving Launch Podcast went live and we quickly received over 40 ratings. This podcast made it on New and Noteworthy on the homepage of itunes and in all 3 of it's categories.

---

77. Luis Congdon - "Lasting Love Connection"

twitter.com/wholesomeunion

Don't be afraid to reach out to your ideal guests. It's easy and since you have a podcast (or about to have one) then you've got a great reason to reach out to your ideal guest. Try this template for conversion magic to get that famous person on your show:

Dear (Name),

I really like x - it's helped me do y.

I have a podcast titled, The Thriving Launch Podcast (insert your show name) and it helps business people launch their business online. (insert what your show does). I'd love to have you on the show to: (write a very brief point that you'd want them to talk about).

The show has had (insert some names - and if you can't name drop, don't do this). The show will go out to thousands (with all your social media accounts, and email you definitely have several thousand that the show will reach).

Being a guest will be simple, we will meet on Skype for 20-30 minutes. We will meet and work around your schedule, all you have to do is show up, I'll record it, edit it, and send out to my audience.

Great! We look forward to having you on the (insert show title).

Thanks,

---

78. Jordan Harbinger -
"The Art of Charm Podcast"

twitter.com/theartofcharm

Don't try to make money podcasting. You're here to be a thought leader, to help others, to share. Monetization should not be the end goal because that will not sustain you through the times when it feels like no one cares about your work.

---

79. Megan Pangan -
"Get in the Lab Video Podcast"

twitter.com/meganjphoto

Get ready for a unexpected, yet awesome journey to self-awareness. Don't edit your umms and uhhs, just be better in the next one.

---

80. Kip Clark - "Stride and Saunter"

twitter.com/StrideNSaunter

Do not worry about your audience size. Make sure that you enjoy your own content first and foremost. Be passionate and genuine with any podcast and the listeners will not only find you, they will stick around for future episodes.

---

81. Blake Soulet - "Fulfilling Life's Yearnings"

twitter.com/BlakeSoulet

I'm sitting alone in my car, as I usually do, on my daily commute to the local Starbucks to do homework, and I was listening to my favorite motivational podcast of the week, The Year of Purpose Podcast with Zephan Moses Blaxberg. Like many of us that listen to podcast, I was simultaneously thinking about what I could to do to take action on my dreams (whatever those are), and then the thought occurred to me...

"Wait a minute, I can do a podcast!" After being overtly excited as I was driving down the road, the thought, "but how," entered my mind. The "how," I found out was simple. Be true to yourself (people love real people) and join a course or find a mentor that will teach you the blueprint for what you need to do run and sustain a podcast that attracts the right people for your show.

---

82. Dr. Jin - "Healthy Positive Lifestyle"

twitter.com/HPLPodcast

I learned from John Maxwell: It is not how high you can jump when you're excited, it is how straight you can walk when you are down. Be consistent and stay your course.

---

83. Alex Harris - "Marketing Optimization"

twitter.com/alexdesigns

In order to understand how to improve your podcast, you need to speak with your listeners. To do this, I would suggest adding an audio call to action for the listen to contact to you. You can do this by asking them to email you or connect with you on Twitter, Facebook or Instagram. After they contact you, get the listen to agree to a Skype call with you.

Schedule the Skype call (I use scheduleonce), record it (to re-listen later) and introduce yourself to the listener and understand how they found you, what they learned from you and what can be improved. Make sure to take the time and give the listener a free consultation or something of extreme value for setting up the Skype call. But you want to understand the language they use to describe the problems in their business, what kinds of things are they doing online and what are their demographics.

More than likely, you are going to see patterns in the people that you will connect with. This is your avatar. Not the listener who you think is subscribed to your show. This is the real listener. You want to find out eveything about them. In order to create content to make their lives and their businesses even better. They will tell you key takeaways that will lead to ideas for new episodes, new products and even new book, courses and videos.

84. David Hooper - "RED Podcast"

twitter.com/davidhooper

Get to the point and keep your episodes short. Most podcasts are consumed in the gym or while commuting and the average time for each is 25 minutes. You will have more success if you can give people a complete episode within that time.

---

85. Mark Eckdahl - "Wisdom From Dads"

twitter.com/meckdahl

Create an I love your podcast page on your website that allows for people to Click on a link to Tweet. You then encourage people who like your podcast to go to "\love" to share the love with a Tweet.

Here is how you do that:

1. Go to Click to Tweet and craft your message (Here is mine):

(clicktotweet.com)
#Love this podcast #WisdomFromDads! Great stories with awesome lessons http://ctt.ec/b9VXK+ pic.twitter.com/PYMNcYjk71

Copy the code provided here to use on your website.

2. Create a WordPress page at (/love), like this:
http://WisdomFromDads.com/love

3. Title the page "Share the Love" and past into the Text editor the code from Click to Tweet. Add any extra formatting/instructions you want!

You tell your audience, "If you like this podcast go to "/love" and give us some Twitter love! It will launch a tweet from their own twitter account with the text you provided as its default. They can customize it, also, if they want to.

---

86. Shimeka Williams - "Design The Life You Want"

twitter.com/shimekism

If you are planning to have an interview-based podcast, know that potential guests are everywhere. If you perceive that attracting guests will be a problem, then it will be. However, if you are always on the lookout for potential guests, then you will find them everywhere.

---

87. Natalie Eckdahl - "Biz Chix Podcast"

twitter.com/bizchixpodcast

Your friends and family will not understand how or why to give you an iTunes review. Tell them it helps you become the podcasting equivalent of an Amazon Bestseller. Create a screencast on how to rate and review. And remember it can take days for a review to show up.

———

88. Steve Lee - "Modern Life Podcast Network"

twitter.com/modernlifepods

Don't try to imitate or be someone you are not. Take a deep breath, let the content stand on its own and be yourself. Podcasting is about individuality not copy cats and hiding behind a virtual facade will only lead to failure.

Know who you are!

———

89. Prescott Perez-Fox - "The Busy Creator Podcast"

twitter.com/scottperezfox

Don't panic — you'll get much better the more you do it. Take it one episode at a time, and even one step at a time in producing that episode.

———

90. John Vonhof - "Writers & Authors on Fire"

Don't panic — you'll get much better the more you do it. Take it one episode at a time, and even one step at a time in producing that episode.

———

91. Kien Tran - "GeekBeat"

twitter.com/kientran

Preproduction is the most important thing to do for a show. Rundowns, pre-editing segments, and even rehearsing all lead to a polished episode that listeners will appreciate.

———

92. Shawn Smith - "The Mobile Pro"

*twitter.com/TheMobilePro_*

Unless you absolutely need it for Skype or live phone calls, avoid a mixer for your mics. Get a USB computer interface - they are much smaller, and much simpler, but will still give you pro-quality audio. And, an interface can handle 1-4 mics for the same price or less than a mixer. Plus, many of them, with a simple Apple Camera Connection Kit, will even allow you to record on the road with an iOS device (iPhone or iPad) as your recorder!

Also, unless you have an extremely quiet space, with lots of soft surfaces to record in, use a DYNAMIC microphone (NOT a

CONDENSER mic). Dynamic mics (i.e. ATR2100USB) are much better at rejecting unwanted room noise (like reverb and echo) and ambient sounds (like household appliances, heating/cooling sounds, clocks, kids, trucks driving by, etc.) But, dynamic mics will still give you pro-quality audio.

Condenser mics are really designed for highly insulated recording studios. They are very sensitive and will pick up lots of unwanted sounds that you'll spend your life trying to edit out, so they are not distracting for your listeners. Save yourself lots of time and headaches by going with a dynamic mic!

---

93. Wayne Henderson - "The Voice-Over Journey"

twitter.com/WayneHenderson

Try not to view other podcasters as "competition". Genuinely befriend and support the other podcasters that are in niches similar to your own. You can build each other up, share some tips, and even appear on each other's shows.

---

94. Todd Uterstaedt - "From Founder To CEO"

twitter.com/fromfounder2ceo

Just get started and refine your audience target as you go along. Much will become clear to you with continued publication of your podcast.

95. Amanda Doughty - "Great Beer Adventure"

twitter.com/greatbeerwomen

Just start! It doesn't matter if you start by just grabbing your cell phone and recording a list of what's in the fridge. Just record something. If you have beer in the fridge you can talk about that and then drink it too. That would be quite lovely and it would get you to just start recording.

96. Hani Mourra - "Simple Podcast Press"

twitter.com/hanimourra

Keep it simple and focus on producing valuable content that has stay power. Don't only focus on what's not now since you listeners will consume your old content for years to come.

97. Jim Munchbach - "#MillionaireBy50"

twitter.com/JimMunchbach

Think outside the box. The podcaster community is an unbelievable resource and there are people in our community – people like Gary Leland – who can help you think outside the box to achieve what matters most.

When I first became a podcaster, I spent a couple of years trying to podcast like other podcasters. At some point, I just gave up. After giving up, I started to ask different questions. I started to think outside the box. In a very short amount of time, I started to gather new information and much better answers to my questions:

- Who is my audience?
- How do I reach them?
- Where do I begin?
- Why do I podcast?

Whenever you start something new, you have to be very careful where you begin. You have to be careful not only about the questions you're asking but the people you are asking to answer your questions.

Today, I'm using my podcast to reach my students at the Bauer College of Business at THE University of Houston. I teach personal finance. And, there's so much I want to teach my students and so little time to achieve the educational objectives.

Podcasting allows me to go far beyond the four walls of our university classroom. When I learned to think outside the box, I was able to move far outside the classroom, too. The community that I am building today will endure for many generations.

I may not know you and I certainly don't know your goals and priorities for creating a podcast. What I do know is this – every human being wants and needs to make a difference.

Podcasting is a lot of work. And, to do it right, there is some expense – some investment. My hope for you is that you will think outside the box, ask better questions, and discover what matters most – to you and your community.

Our podcast community is growing. We have many personalities and a myriad of voices. The future of podcasting involves a whole new realm of possibility for those of us who are willing to do the work and deliver value.

Dial in and Don't give up. Wherever you are today is not where you going to be a year from now. And, imagine where you might be in 10 years after getting very clear about your purpose for podcasting.

———

98. Bryan Orr - "Mantastic Voyage"

twitter.com/BryanJOrr

Set a schedule for when you are going to publish and publish no matter how you feel about what you created. You will only learn from experience and feedback and that can only happen if you publish.

———

99. Chris Doelle - "The Marketing Drive"

twitter.com/chrisdoelle

Record five episodes of your show before you post any of them. Chances are the show intended to create will be slightly different than the one it morphs into. Give yourself time to find your voice and your rhythm. In addition, you will be more comfortable and that will come across in the finished product.

Five shows - no more - no less... that is the magic number. Any less and you will not be ready. Any more and you will risk never get around to launching the show.

———

100. Gary Leland - "The Gary Leland Show"

twitter.com/garyleland

The previous 99 great podcaster's have given you many great tips, but the number one tip I know is to just start! Because you can't improve upon anything until you record the first time.

Good Luck!

Podcast Directories

Having your podcast listed in as many podcast directories as possible is a great way to grow your podcast. It is a great idea to take the time and get your show listed in the places below:

iTunes - www.apple.com/itunes/podcasts/

Stitcher - www.stitcher.com/content-providers

Libsyn - www.libsyn.com/podcast-source-submit/

TuneIn Radio - help.tunein.com/

OverCast App - www.overcast.fm/

All Podcasts - www.allpodcasts.com/Pages/ForPodcasters.aspx

Audio-Podcast.fm - www.audio-podcast.fm/submit-your-podcast.html

Blinkx.tv - www.blinkx.com/rssupload

Blogdigger - www.blogdigger.com/add.jsp

Blubrry - www.blubrry.com/addpodcast.php

BritCaster - www.britcaster.com/user/register.html

CastRoller - www.castroller.com/podcasts/add

Castwing - www.castwing.com/submit-podcast-feed/

DailySplice -
www.dailysplice.com/directory/podcasts/submit

Digital Podcasts - www.digitalpodcast.com/users/sign_in

DJconneXion - www.djconnexion.co.uk/add-listing/

DoubleTwist - www.doubletwist.com/contact/

Fluctu8 - www.fluctu8.com/add-podcast.php

Gigadial - www.gigadial.net/public/

iPodder - www.ipodder.org/hints/new

iTunesTracks.co.uk -
www.itunestracks.co.uk/podcasts/howtosubmit.asp

Learn Out Loud - www.learnoutloud.com/

Lisn.cc - www.lisn.cc/#/upload

OzPodcasts - www.ozpodcasts.com.au/submit/

Player.fm - www.suggest.player.fm/

Plazoo.com - www.plazoo.com/en/addrss.asp

PodBean - www.podbean.com/site/user/login

Podcast411 - www.podcast411.com/

Podcast.de - www.podcast.de/podcastcore/submit/

Podcast.tv - www.podcast.tv/submit-your-podcast.html

Podcast Blaster -
www.podcastblaster.com/directory/add-podcast/

PodcastDirectory -
www.podcastdirectory.com/submit-your-podcast.html

Podcast-Directory.co.uk -
www.podcast-directory.co.uk/submit-your-podcast.html

Podcastellano.com - www.podcastellano.com/

Podcast Pup - www.podcastex.com/addpodcastform.asp

PodcastZoom - www.podcastzoom.com/

PodDirectory - www.poddirectory.com/submit

Podfeed - www.podfeed.net/

PodKicker - www.podkicker.com/submitpodcast.php

Podster.de - www.podster.de/

PublicRadioFan.com -
www.publicradiofan.com/podcasts.html

The Running Podcast List -
www.runningpodcastlist.com/

Two Thumbs Up Media -
www.twothumbsupmedia.com/creator/

Vodcasts.TV - www.videopodcasts.tv/vc.php?action=add

Source:

Full list courtesy of Rob Walch, and *Podcast411.com*

PodSafe Music

This list was compiled to give you sources for podcast safe, music, sound effects, intro's and outro's.

Audio Micro - www.audiomicro.com/free-sound-effects

Creative Commons - search.creativecommons.org

CC Mixter - www.ccmixter.org

GarageBand - www.garageband.com

Incompetech - www.incompetech.com

Ioda Alliance - www.theorchard.com/splash

LoopSound - www.loopsound.com

Magnatune - www.magnatune.com/info/podcast

Music2License - www.music2license.com

Music Buggy - www.musicbuggy.com

Music Loops - www.musicloops.com

Music Track Library - www.musictrackslibrary.com

MySpace - www.myspace.com

Opuzz - www.opuzz.com

PodSafe Audio - www.podsafeaudio.com

PodSafe Music Network - music.podshow.com

Royalty Free Music -
www.royaltyfreemusic.com/music-for-podcasts.htm

Podcast Classical Music -
www.royaltyfreeclassicalmusic.co.uk

SoundClick - www.soundclick.com

Stock Music - www.stockmusic.net

SoundImage.eu - www.soundimage.eu

The BeatSuite - www.beatsuite.com

The Music Bakery - www.musicbakery.com

The Musicase - www.themusicase.com

Podcasting Tools

This list was compiled to give you sources for podcasting tools, software, marketing, analytics, hosting, and editing.

Audio Hosting -

Hosting your audio is an important decision in launching a new podcast. Here is a list of recommended services to get you started on the right track:

Libsyn - www.libsyn.com

Blubrry - www.blubrry.com

BlogTalkRadio - www.blogtalkradio.com

BuzzSprout - www.buzzsprout.com

PowerPress - create.blubrry.com/resources/powerpress

Podbean - www.podbean.com

Soundcloud - www.soundcloud.com

Spreaker - www.spreaker.com

Website Hosting -

This section is for recommended services to host a website and purchase domain names specific to your podcast. These are trusted providers.

Dill Domains - www.dilldomains.com

Bluehost - www.spreaker.com

GoDaddy - www.godaddy.com

Hostgator - www.hostgator.com

Website Builder -

For creating your own website with themes, plugins, opt-ins and more.

Wordpress - www.wordpress.org

Squarespace - www.squarespace.com

Rainmaker - www.rainmakerplatform.com

Tracking & Analytics -

Use of a service like PodTrac will allow you to mask your RSS Feed through their Tracking service and then submit an enhanced feed to podcatchers.

PodTrac - www.podtrac.com

Feed Validator - www.feedvalidator.org

Recording -

The programs and apps below are a great way to start recording and editing audio. A few listed are used to record interviews over the web with another person.

Audacity - www.audacityteam.org

Adobe Audition -
www.creative.adobe.com/products/audition

Audio Hijack - www.rogueamoeba.com/audiohijack

Blab - www.blab.im

Boss Jock Studio - www.bossjockstudio.com

Garageband - www.apple.com/mac/garageband

Google Hangouts - plus.google.com/hangouts

Skype - www.skype.com/en

Pamela for Skype - www.pamela.biz

Recordium - www.recordiumapp.com

SoundForge -
www.sonycreativesoftware.com/soundforgesoftware

Total Recorder - www.totalrecorder.com

Audio Tools -

Here are a few tools recommended from the podcast community. Some are for use to improve your final audio quality. Other's can be useful to play triggered sound effects or embed an audio player in your website.

Auphonic - www.auphonic.com

Levelator - www.conversationsnetwork.org/levelator

Simple Podcast Press - www.simplepodcastpress.com/

Smart Podcast Player - www.smartpodcastplayer.com

SoundByte - Radio Styled Soundboard App
www.blackcatsystems.com/download/soundbyte.html

SpeakPipe - Voice Mail Recording On Your Website
www.speakpipe.com/

Artwork -

Use these simple web apps to create images, social media images with text, cover art, and more.

Canva - www.canva.com/

Pic Monkey - www.picmonkey.com

Pixlr - www.pixlr.com

Email Marketing - Used to create mailing lists, automated newsletters, subscription lists and more.

AWebber - www.aweber.com

Mail Chimp - www.mailchimp.com

Social Media Tools -

Used to create automated posts, analytics, and more.

Facebook - www.facebook.com
Has built in scheduling capabilities through your podcast admin page.

Sprout Social - www.sproutsocial.com -
Used to track, schedule, and tracking of your posts to several social media platform.

Latergram.Me - www.latergram.me -
Used to create and schedule posts for Instagram

Buffer - www.buffer.com -
Buffer is the easiest way to publish on social media.

Hoot Suite - www.hootsuite.com -
Get the world's #1 platform for managing social media.

IFTTT - www.ifttt.com -

Connect the apps you love, create recipes for behind the scenes automation of everyday tasks.

Podcasts About Podcasting

Ask the Podcast Coach - www.askthepodcastcoach.com

Cashflow Podcasting - www.cashflowpodcasting.com

Podcast Junkies - www.podcastjunkies.com

Podcast Talent Coach - www.podcasttalentcoach.com

Podcast Answerman - www.podcastanswerman.com

Podcast Help Desk - www.podcasthelpdesk.com

Podcasters Roundtable - www.podcastersroundtable.com

Podcaster's Group Therapy - www.podcastersgrouptherapy.com

Podcastification - www.podcastfasttrack.com/category/podcast

Podcasting101 - www.podcasting101.libsyn.com

Pod on Pod - www.teamprocreate.com/podcasts/pod-pod

Profitcast - www.profitcastuniverse.com

School of Podcasting - www.schoolofpodcasting.com

She Podcasts - www.shepodcasts.com

The Podcaster's Studio - www.thepodcastersstudio.com

The Podcast Report - www.thepodcastreport.com

The Podcast Reporter - www.podcastreporter.com

The Audacity to Podcast -
www.theaudacitytopodcast.com

The Show Runner -
www.rainmaker.fm/series/showrunner

The Feed - www.thefeed.libsyn.com

Wolf Den - www.earwolf.com/show/wolf-den

My Resources

Podertainment

The Podcast Magazine

Since there was not a magazine for podcasting, I decided to publish a podcast magazine. I drew on my past experience publishing my first magazine, a sports niche devoted to all areas of Fastpitch Softball.

This magazine contains a ton of great information for such a small amount of money. Podertainment will have 12 issues a year, and will release the middle of every month. A subscription to Podertainment is $12.99 a year.

www.Podertainment.com

PodcastJunk

Your Online Source for Podcast Gear!

Dedicated to bringing you some of the best deals on some of my favorite podcast equipment and resources. I bring you access to my growing network of partnerships with top of the line podcast equipment companies. I have reviewed podcast gear over the years and can recommend excellent options for the beginner to the advanced podcaster.

Gary Leland Show

I encourage you to join me as I sit down with industry experts and pick their brain on several of the top online industry platforms. Past guests include Chris Brogan on Marketing, Dennis Yu and Alex Houg on Facebook, Cynthia Sanchez on Pinterest, Gary's Personal Facebook Strategy, Paul Colligan on Marketing, David Jackson on Podcasting, Jeremy Vest on YouTube, Tim Paige on Leadpages, Lynette Young on Aweber, Patrick Rauland on Woo Commerce, and many more! I am confident listening to these interviews will be time well spent.

www.GaryLelandShow.com

E-Book

Marketing Your Retail Store in an Online World Vol. 1

By Gary Leland

I wanted to ask some of the best minds in the online industry how using social media and multicasting will help you sell actual products. When I say selling products, I'm not talking about selling ebooks, or webinars, or online conferences, I am talking about selling real, physical products. Things you may inventory or ship to your customers; maybe its shoes, maybe jewelry, or softball equipment like I do. Whatever your reasons, I know you will gain knowledge and insight into running a successful e-commerce business.

www.GaryLeland.com/Book

Softball Websites

20 Years Experience Building Websites!

My name is Gary Leland, and I have been involved with fastpitch softball for many years, but I have been creating websites even longer. I created my first e-commerce site in 1996, my first podcast in 2004, and in 2006 Time Magazine included one of my websites in their 50 coolest websites of the year. Today I run over 20 websites of my own, and build websites for other.

I also am a pioneer in the world of podcasting. I was one of the first 100 podcaster in the world. My first podcast went live in 2004, and my first video podcast went live in 2006. My videos have been viewed millions of times on YouTube, and almost as many on Facebook.

Over the years so many people have asked me who they should contact to get a website, podcast, or even social media projects built, and I never knew who to recommend. Finally I decided that I would start helping people with their projects, and Softball Websites was born.

www.SoftballWebsites.com

Podcast Dallas

Podcast Meetup Group

This is a monthly meet up dedicated to helping grow the world of podcasting in Dallas, TX. Once a month Podcast Dallas supplies resources to podcasters to share their skills, and gain a wealth of valuable information. This group will bring you knowledgable presenters as well as hosting a growing environment of networking opportunities.

www.PodcastDallas.com

Podcast Movement

The #1 Podcast Conference

In August 2015, over 1,000 past, present, and future podcasters converged on the Omni Hotel Fort Worth for two packed days and nights at the second annual Podcast Movement. Podcast Movement 2015 was THE gathering for anyone interested in podcasting. Don't miss another chance to attend the biggest podcast event of the year.

The founders are excited to announce that Podcast Movement 2016 is coming to the windy city, Chicago! Join over 1,000 of your closest podcasting friends and the best podcasters in the world! You can expect to find a place where not only will you leave motivated and inspired, you'll leave a BETTER PODCASTER.

www.PodcastMovement.com

Notes

Conclusion

I hope you found the information provided in this book to be helpful suggestions, great advice, and tools to help you launch, grow, and monetize your podcast. Each person who contributed their knowledge to this book is a trusted friend of mine and has had success in their podcast at every level of the industry. If podcasting is your passion, take this advice and run with it!

Best Regards,

Gary Leland

CPSIA information can be obtained
at www.ICGtesting.com
Printed in the USA
LVOW04s1840030316

477651LV00028B/966/P